I0814448

HELICOPTERS

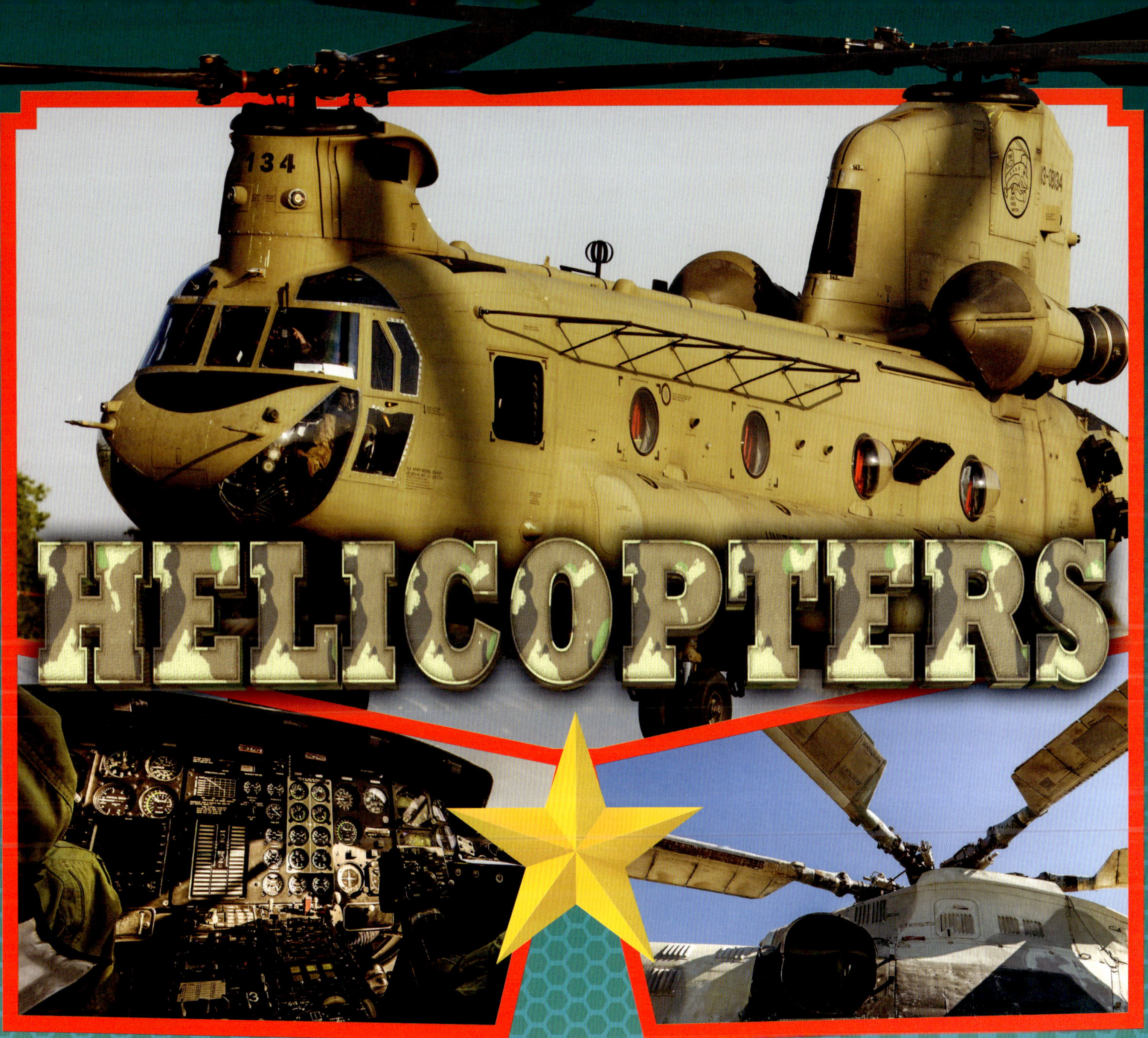

John Willis

AV2
www.openlightbox.com

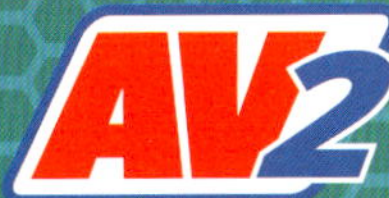

Step 1
Go to **www.openlightbox.com**

Step 2
Enter this unique code
EIPYFB8U7

Step 3
Explore your interactive eBook!

MEGA MILITARY MACHINES
AV2
HELICOPTERS
Start!
Share

AV2 is optimized for use on any device

Your interactive eBook comes with...

Audio
Listen to the entire book read aloud

Videos
Watch informative video clips

Weblinks
Gain additional information for research

Try This!
Complete activities and hands-on experiments

Key Words
Study vocabulary, and complete a matching word activity

Quizzes
Test your knowledge

Slideshows
View images and captions

Share
Share titles within your Learning Management System (LMS) or Library Circulation System

Citation
Create bibliographical references following APA, CMOS, and MLA styles

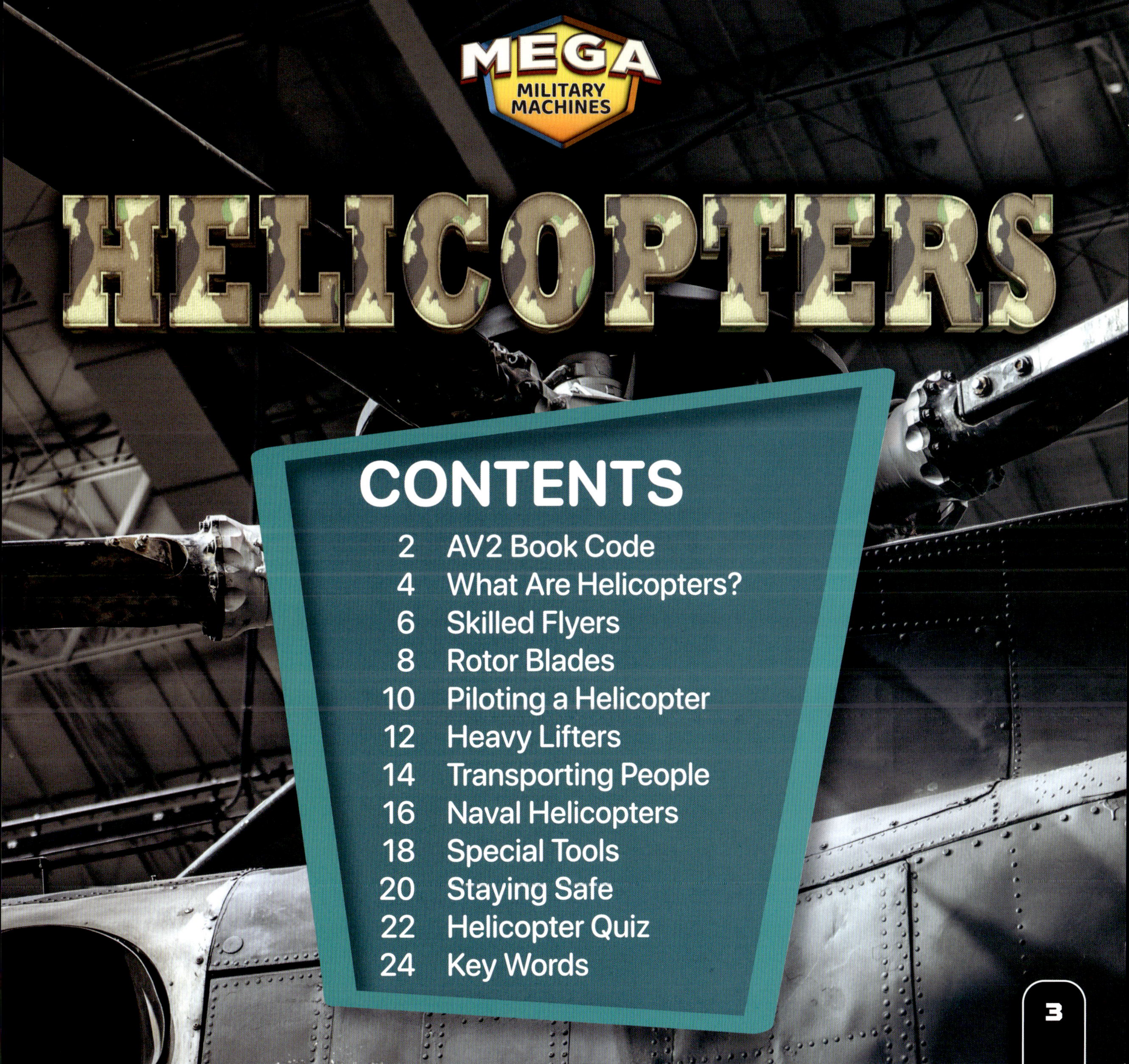

HELICOPTERS

CONTENTS

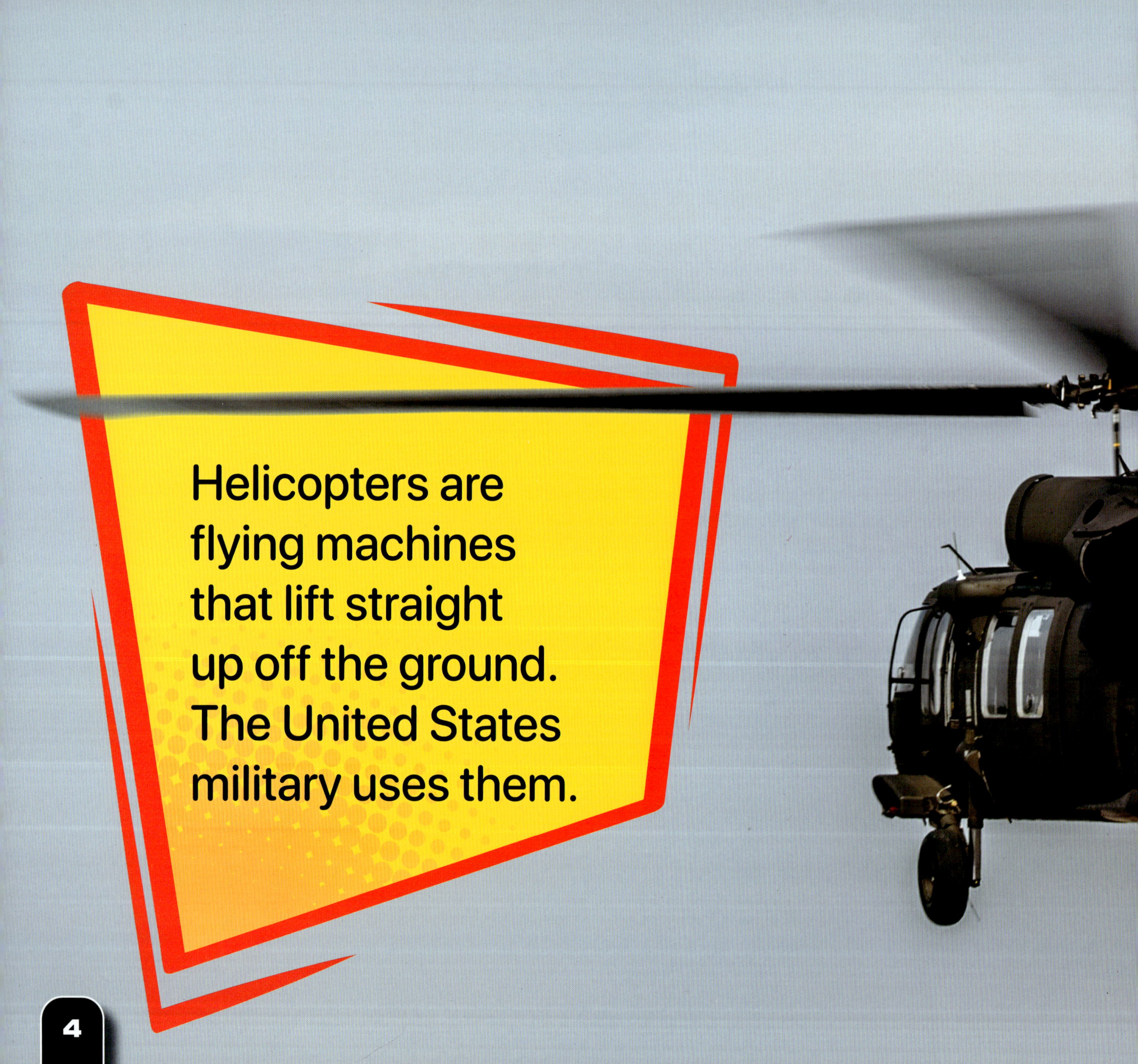

Helicopters are flying machines that lift straight up off the ground. The United States military uses them.

FAMOUS U.S. MILITARY HELICOPTERS

1944
R-4

1979
UH-60 Black Hawk

1986
AH-64 Apache

Helicopters can fly in every direction. They can even fly backward.

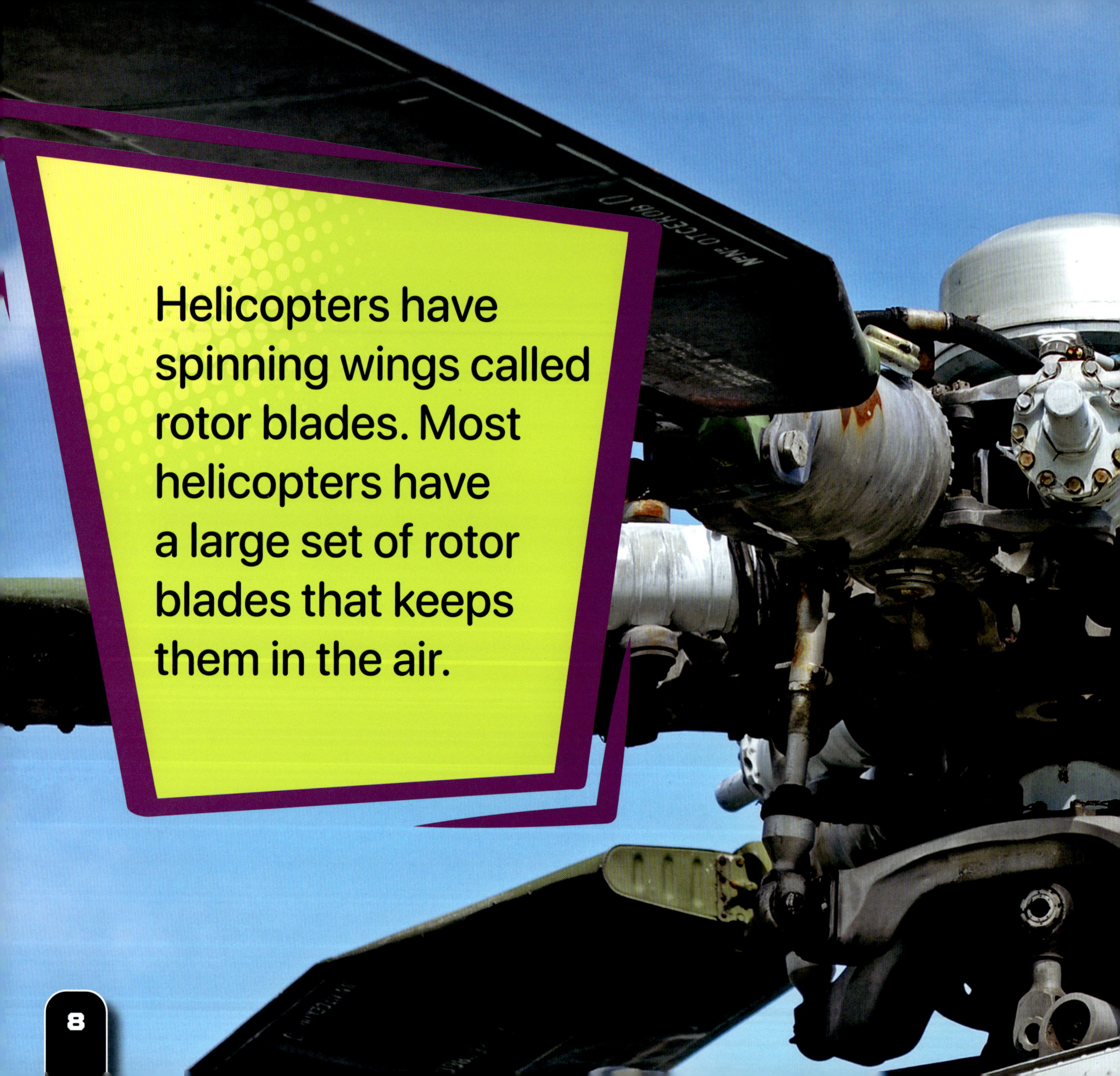

Helicopters have spinning wings called rotor blades. Most helicopters have a large set of rotor blades that keeps them in the air.

COMPARING HELICOPTER BLADES
Bell UH-1 Iroquois
2 large rotor blades
Bell AH-17 Viper
4 large rotor blades
Sikorsky CH-53E Super Stallion
7 large rotor blades

A pilot flies the helicopter from the cockpit. Levers help the pilot control its speed and direction.

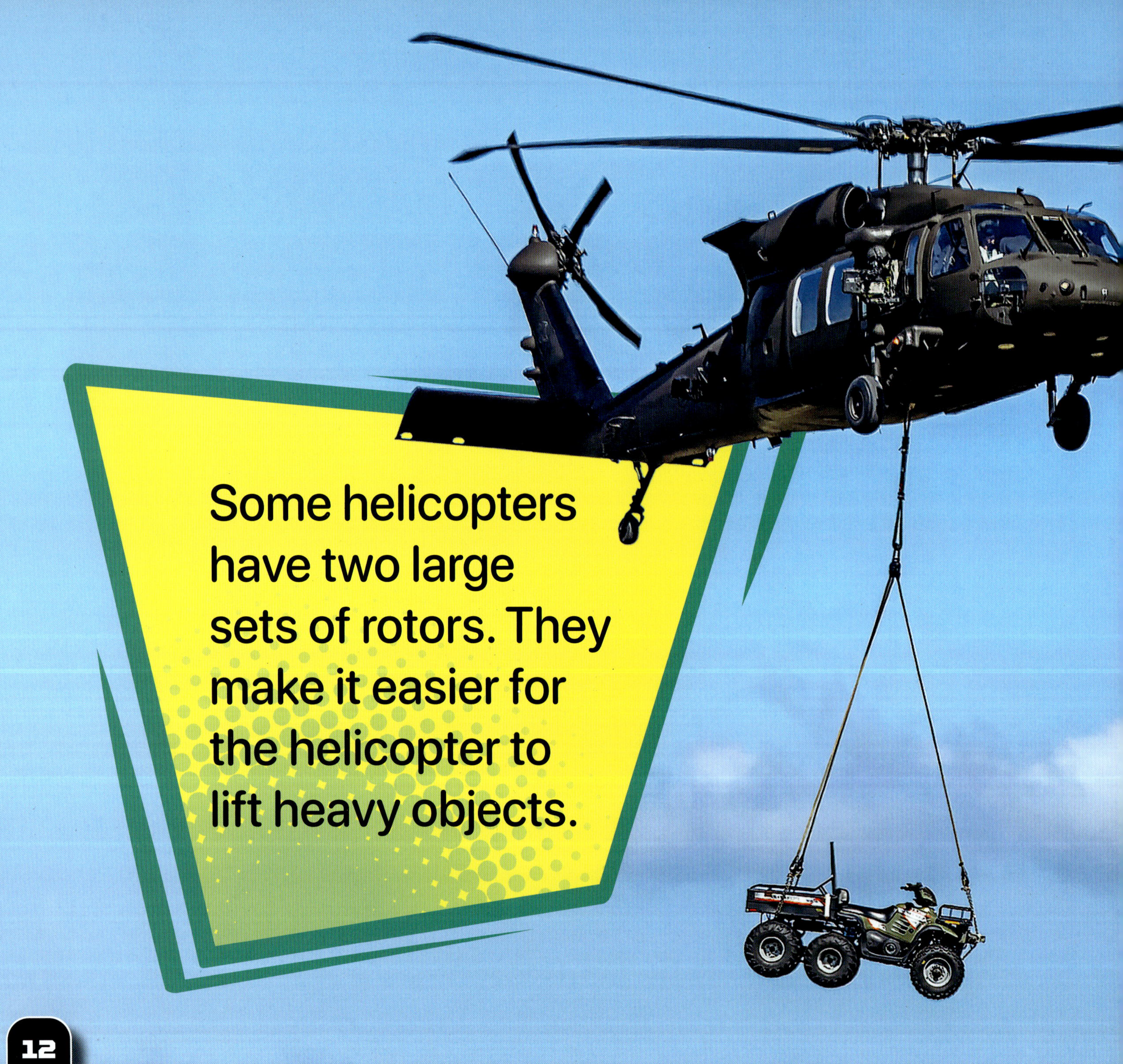

Some helicopters have two large sets of rotors. They make it easier for the helicopter to lift heavy objects.

Some Chinook helicopters are large enough to hold vehicles. They can also carry heavy loads under them.

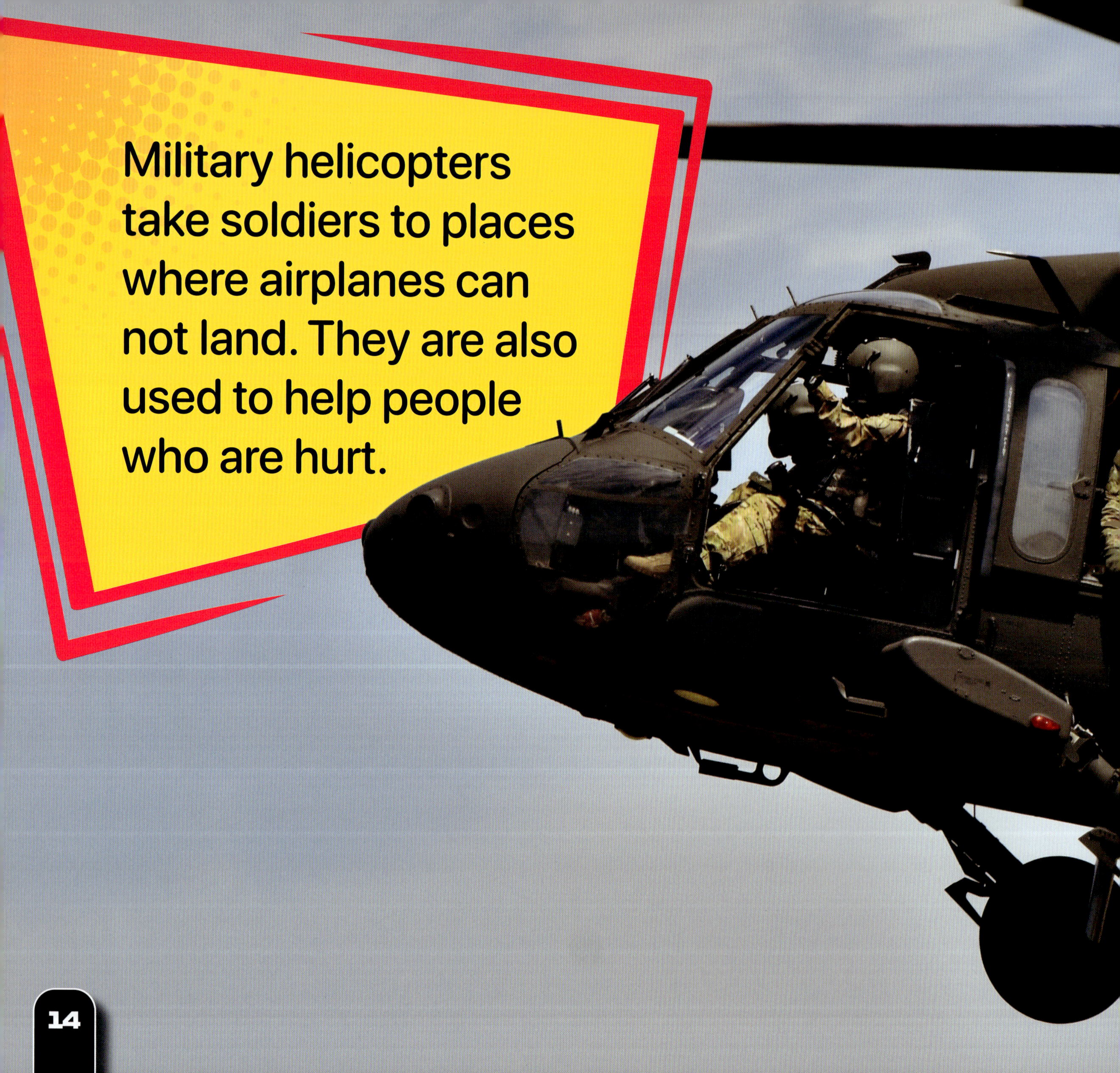

Military helicopters take soldiers to places where airplanes can not land. They are also used to help people who are hurt.

A Black Hawk helicopter can carry up to 11 soldiers at once.

The U.S. Navy uses helicopters to protect ships from attacks. Naval helicopters can also be used to help people in the water.

Military helicopters may have special tools, such as radar. Radar lets pilots know if other helicopters or airplanes are nearby.

Some Apache helicopters can spot 256 objects with their radar in only 30 seconds.

The U.S. military uses helicopters around the world. They help keep people safe.
TYPES
OF U.S. MILITARY
HELICOPTERS
Attack
Transport
Utility

Maritime
Search and Rescue
Observation

See what you have learned about helicopters.

Which of these pictures does not show a helicopter?
704

KEY WORDS

Research has shown that as much as 65 percent of all written material published in English is made up of 300 words. These 300 words cannot be taught using pictures or learned by sounding them out. They must be recognized by sight. This book contains 59 common sight words to help young readers improve their reading fluency and comprehension. This book also teaches young readers several important content words, such as proper nouns. These words are paired with pictures to aid in learning and improve understanding.

Page	Sight Words First Appearance
4	are, off, states, that, the, them, up, uses
6	can, even, every, in, they
8	a, air, have, keeps, large, most, of, set
10	and, from, its
12	for, it, make, some, to, two
13	also, carry, enough, under
14	land, not, people, places, take, where, who
15	at, once
17	be, water
18	as, if, know, lets, may, or, other, such
19	only, seconds, their, with
20	around, world

Page	Content Words First Appearance
4	ground, helicopters, machines, military, United States
5	AH-64 Apache, R-4, UH-60 Black Hawk
6	direction
8	rotor blades, set, wings
9	Bell AH-17 Viper, Bell UH-1 Iroquois, Sikorsky CH-53E Super Stallion
10	cockpit, levers, pilot, speed
12	objects
13	Chinook, loads, vehicles
14	airplanes, soldiers
17	attacks, ships, U.S. Navy
18	radar, tools
20	Attack, Transport, Utility
21	Maritime, Observation, Search and Rescue

Published by Lightbox Learning Inc.
276 5th Avenue, Suite 704 #917
New York, NY 10001
Website: www.openlightbox.com

Library of Congress Control Number: 2023931795

ISBN 978-1-7911-5538-4 (hardcover)
ISBN 978-1-7911-5539-1 (softcover)
ISBN 978-1-7911-5540-7 (multi-user eBook)

Printed in Guangzhou, China
1 2 3 4 5 6 7 8 9 0 27 26 25 24 23

042023
100922

Project Coordinator: Priyanka Das **Designer:** Terry Paulhus

Every reasonable effort has been made to trace ownership and to obtain permission to reprint copyright material. The publisher would be pleased to have any errors or omissions brought to its attention so that they may be corrected in subsequent printings.

The publisher acknowledges Getty Images, Shutterstock, the U.S. Air Force, the U.S. Navy, and Wikimedia as the primary image suppliers for this title.